God's Guidance Through Poetry

by

Neal A. Carl

ISBN: 1-4140-4119-5 (e-book)
ISBN: 1-4140-4118-7 (Paperback)

Printed in the United States of America
Bloomington, IN

This book is printed on acid free paper.

1st Books - rev. 01/07/04

Dedications

This book of poems is dedicated in Praise to God the Father, for loving me so much he sent his son, Jesus, to die on the cross at Mt. Calvary for me.

In Praise to my Lord and Savior, Jesus Christ, who loves me so much, He died on that cross for my sins. A cross that should have been mine, but he willingly took my place.

And to the Holy Spirit who guides me and teaches me daily, giving direction to become more like Jesus, my Lord and Savior, the Son of God!

Acknowledgments

To my parents, for raising me in a good Christian home and answering God's call to teach their children about Jesus' sacrifice for us.

To my brother and sisters, for their continued support and encouragement of my poetry gift from God and for their love.

To my loving wife, who's love, encouragement, and sacrifice during the writing and publishing of this book, and for her shared belief that these poems are inspired by God.

To my girls, who give me much joy and will also serve the Lord.

Dear Reader,

At a time in my life when God was reaching out to me, to give me the guidance I had been praying for, He gave me the inspiration to write these poems.

As I wrote each poem, I soon realized that God was using these poems (messages) to give me guidance. The more I read his word and came to Him in prayer, the closer my walk with Jesus became and the more the words flowed.

My prayer for you is that these poems will help guide you as much as they have me to a closer walk. As we read God's word, The Holy Bible, we will see these poems are an expression of the love and guidance He gives as we learned to grow closer to Him.

In Christ,

Neal A. Carl

Table of Contents

Son of God -- 1
Jesus is the Answer --- 2
To Follow Jesus --- 3
The Son Still Shines -- 4
Close to You --- 5
The Holy Spirit -- 6
I Cry -- 7
From Death on a Cross --- 9
To Serve Christ --- 10
The Cure --- 11
The Street Dwellers -- 12
Unchanged! -- 13
Jail Ministry --- 14
The Shoe Box God -- 15
Count Your Blessings --- 16
Freedom --- 17
The Master's Voice --- 18
Missed the Message -- 19
I Am the Potter --- 20
When God Speaks -- 21
Climb Every Mountain --- 22
Troubled by Storms -- 23
The Narrow Road --- 24
Seen My Scars -- 25
The Lighthouse -- 26
Sins Forgiven --- 27
My Love Overflows --- 28
My Temple --- 29
Reborn and Transformed -- 30
Lost Cause or Saved! -- 31
Check Yourself -- 32
A Matter of Time --- 33
Life Goes On -- 34
Show My Love --- 36
Feeling Condemned -- 37
Broken the Law --- 38
Your Turn Now -- 39
Will You Obey? -- 40
What's Next? --- 41

Sheltered in the Lord -- 42
When Temptation Comes -- 43
Overpowered by Fear -- 44
No More Pain --- 45
Are You Listening? -- 46
What If? --- 47
Praise the Lord -- 48
Jesus is Coming -- 49
A Prayer by Jesus -- 50
Seeds of Faith -- 51
Hourglass Design -- 52
Stand Together -- 53
He Has Risen -- 54
Worship Me! -- 55
I Have Risen --- 56
Out of Control --- 57
It's Your Choice --- 58
A Sinner's Testimony --- 59
This is the Day --- 60
One Victory at a Time -- 61
Do It His Way -- 62
Your Mission --- 63
No Time to Waste --- 64
Whose Choice Is It? --- 65
God's Written Word --- 66
Simple Blessings --- 67
What A Day! -- 68
The Battle is Over --- 69
The Gift of Love --- 70
Do You Remember? -- 71
Monster Slayer -- 72
Answer the Call --- 73

Son of God

The Son of God,
Is very true.
He's always around to keep,
An eye upon you.
He died on the cross,
To take away our sins.
When you accept Him,
Your new life begins.
He defeated Satan in the
Battle at the cross.
And for Satan,
It was a great loss.
For Christ is the Son of God!
His life battle,
Was against temptation.
But He won the battle,
To give us a new salvation.
He is a special cure.
For if you believe in Him;
When God looks through Him,
We are made pure!
He was born of Mary,
It was Christ Jesus,
That she carried.
The Son of God,
Is also the word.
Believe in Him,
And everlasting life,
Is assured!

4/1/1979

Neal A. Carl

Jesus is the Answer

God knew we needed someone,
To help us walk, the daily road.
Someone to encourage us,
And ease our burdened load.
Someone to pick us up,
When we fall.
To help us through our
Fears and all.
Jesus is His answer.

God knew we needed someone,
To cleanse us from our sin.
But to cleanse our heart and mind,
He would have to start from within.
Jesus is His answer.

To surrender to His direction,
This we would have to do.
If we were to find correction,
And forgiveness of our sins too.
We must ask Jesus into our heart,
Be born again--- made a new.
Jesus is His answer.

Yes Jesus is the answer,
For the world today.
Above Him there is no other,
Jesus is the only way.

Sept. 16, 2002

2

To Follow Jesus

To follow Jesus our Lord,
Is sometimes a hard road.
You may get treated badly,
And carry a heavy burden load.
The trials you face,
May seem too large.
But His love and grace,
Will help with your charge.
To run the race,
And finish for the prize.
Oh to leave this place,
And live forever at His side.
Many changes we must go through,
And tasks are asked to do.
Helping us to grow,
So in the future;
His will we may know.
Our old self,
Must be cast away.
So that our new life,
Will forever stay.
His crimson blood,
Covered up our sins.
So that these changes,
Can come from within.
The road is narrow,
And sometimes steep.
His promise to save us,
We know He will keep.
So as you go along,
This winding pathway.
Praise the Lord,
In word and song.
Stay focused above,
And your faith,
Will remain strong.

10/18/2002

Neal A. Carl

The Son Still Shines

Though he was born
In a lowly place,
He was sent by God
Light radiated from his face.
The shepherds came
And the wise men too,
God's son will shine
This they all knew.
As He grew up
He spent his time,
Teaching to all people
Healing the sick and blind.
Many miracles He did
So God's glory could be seen,
Yet the death he endured
Was cruel and mean.
He died with loud thunder,
Was His message to end?
He rose in three days
Just as He had said.
He came to many
To show He was alive,
Then ascended to heaven
And sat at God's side.
After all these years
His message is still true,
He died on that cross
For both me and you.

Jesus the Son Still Shines!

10/19/2002

Close to You

Close to You
Is where I want to be.
Cleansed by your blood
From sin, set free.

To talk with You
And have strong faith,
Ever ready to serve
Be molded as clay.

Your loving sacrifice
I can't ever repay,
Stay close to me
Each night and day.

Someday soon
I will see your face,
When home in heaven
I receive your grace.

10/19/2002

Neal A. Carl

The Holy Spirit

The Holy Spirit
Will fill your heart.
But asking Jesus in,
Is the place to start.

He'll guide you on,
The way you must go.
And through you plant,
The seeds He'll make grow.

He'll give you conviction,
Your sins He'll make known.
Forgiveness you'll seek,
His light in you shown.

Your troubles and cares,
Will soon disappear.
As you focus on God,
Each day of the year.

So listen to His voice,
As trials come your way.
And you'll make the right choice,
As you walk with Him each day.

10/24/2002

I Cry

When I think of
All the homeless,
Who walk the streets
With feelings of hopelessness.
I cry!
When I think of
All the starving people,
Who have had food supplies
Stolen by governments of evil.
I cry!
When I think of those
Who have died in wars,
And never heard Jesus' knocking
At their hearts doors.
I cry!
When I think of the
Tragedies of nine-eleven,
And consider all those
Who may not have gone to heaven?
I cry!
When I think of God's love
And mercy for the lost,
That He sent his son Jesus
To die on my cross.
I cry!
Such a loving God
Cares for you and me,
Too many hardened hearts
Who refuse to be set free.
I cry!
When I think of all the lost
Who have gone to hell's grave,
Because we as Christians
Have become the world's slaves.
I cry!
If only everyone, would accept
They need Jesus to be free from sin.
To Thee oh Lord, I'd cry with praise
Great rejoicing from with-in.

11/06/2002

From Death on a Cross

***Can you imagine
Death on a cross?***

Nailed to the crossbeam,
All your blood loss.
Your body gets heavy
Pulling at your hands.
Every skeletal muscle
Stretching like rubber bands.
The weight of your body
Becomes too heavy to bear.
You cringe with pain
As your wounds start to tear.
The sun's hot rays
Just beating you down.
Can't get any relief,
Skin just burning brown.
Left there to die
For all to see.
Please God let it end!
Is your breathless plea.
Your strength is gone,
Nothing more to give.
The sweat and blood drips,
Like sand through a sieve.
After you have died
The crowd will soon go.

Your body is taken down
Covered with cloths head to toe.
God sent his son
To die in this way.
Bringing Him back to life,
He did rise the third day.
He appeared to many
So they could see.
He had overcome death
From the grave, been set free.
This was God's plan
For the forgiveness of our sins.
We must claim Jesus as Lord
Then the salvation process begins.
As you grow in Jesus
The Holy Spirit will fill you.
Each day you'll see changes
As your life is made new.
Soon we'll see God's promise
Of love, mercy and grace.
And one day ascend to heaven,
Welcomed home to His smiling
face.

11/11/2002

Neal A. Carl

To Serve Christ

To serve the Lord Jesus,
In all that you do.
Reading His word daily,
He will speak to you.

You'll witness to those,
Who may have been lost.
Reaching out everywhere,
Whatever the cost.

Maybe in the jails,
Or out on the streets.
Right in your neighborhood,
Where ever you may meet.

When you follow God's plan,
Things will fall into place.
As you share Jesus with others,
You'll see changes in their face.

Expressions of great joy,
May follow with tears.
They receive forgiveness of sins,
And let go of their fears.

You'll feel the blessings,

Being used as God's tool,
When you accept his direction,
To the harvesting pool.

"I will make you fishers of men"
The Lord Jesus has said.
"I'll take care of your needs,
And give you your daily bread".

So serve the Lord Jesus,
With all of your heart.
Blessings will be overflowing,
He'll show you where to start.

Be persistent in prayer,
Giving thanks to God.
For taking you where others,
May be afraid to trod.

11/16/2002

**Refer to
Colossians Chapters 1-4
Paul's letter to the Colossians**

10

The Cure

You seek a physician
When you are sick.
Or look to a friend
When troubles seem thick.

We look for help,
When we need a hand.
Or just someone to,
Listen and understand.

But there is one sickness,
With no earthly cure.
It's our sin against God
We've all done it for sure!

Whether your sin is big,
Or may even seem small.
Just too many of them,
You can't list them all.

Confess them to Jesus
He'll forgive you your sin.
He is sin's only cure.
Jesus heals you from within.

11/17/2002

Neal A. Carl

The Street Dwellers

Have you ever given thought,
Of those who live on the street?
The ones who seem so dirty,
You walk around not to meet.
They sleep where ever,
A place can be found.
In a box, park bench,
Or an alley on the ground.
They are just people,
Like you and me.
Who want a better life,
In this land of the free.
But for one reason,
Or many others,
They don't get help,
From a sister or brother.
Whether red, yellow,
Black or white,
They are special,
In Jesus' sight.
In this great country,
With its flags unfurled.
We must learn to love,
All the people of the world.

Jesus' death on the cross,
Wasn't just for me and you.
He died for all people,
The street dwellers too!
So ask yourselves,
"What can I do?"
Maybe some clothes,
Or give them some food.
If we pray to God,
And ask where to start.
He'll answer our prayer,
And enlighten our heart.
Dear, Lord give us courage,
To go where you ask.
Supply us with wisdom,
Accompany us on the task.
Give us direction, oh God,
So that we may,
Tell them about Jesus,
And help in some way.

11/17/2002

Unchanged!

From the day you accepted,
Jesus as Lord and Savior.
In His word we read,
We must change our behavior.
It's true when we confessed,
Our sins to the Lord.
They are all wiped away,
And remembered no more.
Change we must go through,
The old self lives no more.
We must now live for Jesus,
To get through heavens door.
If we continue to live,
As we have in the past.
A slap in the face of Jesus,
Is what we have cast.
When the Pharisees brought to
Jesus,
The woman found in sexual sin.
Jesus said" *I do not condemn you,
Go, but do not sin again"*.
The Holy Spirit within us,
We received to guide us through.

These earthly trials and tribulations,
The narrow road, straight and true.
We are to be changed by faith,
And passionately serve the Lord.

To remain in a life unchanged,
Is one we can not afford.
To become more like Jesus,
This is his command.
So if you are unchanged,
Just where do you stand?
Are you standing for Jesus,
And growing in the spirit.
Or has your life stayed unchanged,
Because his voice, you can't hear
it.
These questions must be
answered,
By those of you with doubt.
I tell you, life apart from Jesus,
Is one I can do without.
Changed or unchanged.
Just where do you fall?
Give your all for Jesus,
At the cross, he gave all.

11/23/2002

Refer to Romans 13: 9-14

Neal A. Carl

Jail Ministry

So many lost souls,
Are in our jails.
A life of crime,
Both male and females.
Many are very young,
And some quite old.
Their trouble filled lives,
Created hearts of stone.
These people need to hear,
What JESUS did for them.
So their lives can be changed,
Hearts of stone, turned to gem.
They need to hear,
Of His forgiveness and love.
That He died on the cross,
Cleansed their sins, with His blood.
To hear of His teachings,
And the miracles He did.
The raising from the dead,
Of Lazarus and Jarisus' kid.
The chance to make,
An important decision.
To accept the free gift,
CHRIST as LORD, salvation.
If you hear GOD'S calling,
To a ministry like this.
Serve, giving your whole self,
The cleansing blood was His!

11/23/2002

The Shoe Box God

It seems so many Christians,
Who are weak in faith.
Think GOD is someone,
They can keep in one place.

Some think He is there,
For their every whim.
That whatever they ask for,
They will get it from Him.

But GOD is much more,
Than we will ever know.
He created the world,
It's beauty to show.

He made man in His image,
Every animal, tree, and such.
Even sent His Son JESUS to die,
Because He loved us so much.

GOD says to ask for,
Whatever we may need.
But the question remains,

Do we need it indeed?

He is the great " I AM,"
He's not someone's genie.
To give them three wishes,
So they look good in a bikini.

He created us for His use,
To serve Him however.
To grow in His Spirit,
He will love us forever.

So open the shoe box,
And let Father GOD out.
He is always close by,
You don't need to shout.

Put your trust in Him,
And your faith will grow.
You will learn so much,
And many wonders be shown.

11/24/02

Neal A. Carl

Count Your Blessings

Have you ever counted your blessings,
And named them one by one.
Has the first blessing thought of,
Been *GOD'S* gift of his *SON.*

Have you thought of all,
JESUS has done for you.
The love and happiness you feel,
The changes in life you've gone through.

The things in your past,
He helps you stay away from.
And the new life you're living,
With Him, how far you've come.

Each days blessing of walking with Him,
Sharing time with family and friends,
Blessings of home, work, leisure,
Helping others, health, it never ends.

The blessings overflow the banks,
As a river crests to flood.
Let *JESUS* live and work through you,
The blessings flow like his blood.

So count your blessings,
Even if you can't name them all.
And when Satan attacks you,
Cling to *JESUS* and you won't fall.

11/28/2002

Freedom

Through out the years,
There have always been wars.
People fighting for freedom,
Dead bodies keeping score.

Fights between countries,
Some between faiths.
Even more for piles of dirt,
Or the name of some place.

There seems to be conflict,
For just about any reason.
Many don't know why,
Or care what season.

If only all people,
Would try to understand.
There is only one GOD,
He created sky, sea, and land.

He sacrificed his only Son,
To give us forgiveness of sin.
If you seek true freedom,
Accept JESUS as Lord to begin.

11/29/2002

Neal A. Carl

The Master's Voice

Do you hear
The masters voice?

Giving you direction,
And also a choice.

Asking you to serve,
Telling you where to go.
Sustaining you for the task,
Imparting wisdom to know.

Supplying all your needs,
Getting to the destination.
Giving you the power,
To overcome procrastination.

As you read GOD'S word,
For your lesson of the day.
Filling you with the spirit,
Telling you what to say.

So listen for His voice,
As you go along the way.
He'll help you through rough times,
And by your side He will stay.

12/05/2002

Missed the Message

At one time I thought, I had learned so much.
But during this past year, God has shown I'm out of touch.
All of my forty-four years, I've been raised in the church.
Little did I really notice, being lost in my search.
There is safety in numbers; this was my false belief.
That hanging with church members, was a sigh of relief.
Being with my fellow believers, to help me spiritually grow.
I thought I would learn much, but little did I know.
There were so many Christians, stalled in their faith walk.
You wouldn't know they were saved, the way they would talk!
Their life was no witness, for me to try and follow.
Somehow they missed the message;
their faith seemed so hollow.
Instead of growing up, I was being knocked down.
By not catching on sooner, I had almost drowned.
But God reached out to me, and showed me my faults.
Believing that all fellowship wouldn't bring such results.
Now God is showing me, each day I read his word.
Keep my hearts-eye on Him, and act wisely on what's heard.
So many other Christians lost in life's desert.
Missing God's soft prompting, not hearing Him, not alert.
Live to be more like Jesus, once we've been forgiven.
Being molded into new life,
changing our ways, no more sinnen.
It's true we may fall, every now and then.
But not committing the same sin, time and time again.
We must live to serve God, let the Holy Spirit lead us.
Through the changes we must make, to be more like Jesus.
So listen to God's message, don't miss out on his promise.
Pray and read His word daily, don't follow a doubting Thomas!

12/30/2002

19

Neal A. Carl

I Am the Potter

And God said to me:
I am the potter, and you are the clay.
I will mold and shape you, in my own special way.
You have been washed, by the blood.
Of the sacrificial lamb, who is my Son.
I will teach you, and train you to be.
A blessing and witness to others,
So that they will know me.
A willing servant you must become.
I want to save all, not just one.
You have shed your past life,
Keeping your eyes focused above.
So I can fill you with my Spirit,
And you can pass on my love.
Be kind and compassionate,
Sharing the gospel with all.
I want all the people to hear,
And don't want any to fall.
But the people still have,
Freedom to make a choice.
To love life in this world,
Or to seek me and follow my voice.
I created all people,
In the same image as my own.
Not as a robot, or a mechanical drone.
My Son paid the price,
For the sinful way you've been living.
And even though He is without sin,
He died in your place, His life freely giving.
My Son will wash away your sins,
When you confess Him as Savior and Lord.
Your sins will be buried in the deepest sea,
Vanished, Forgotten, Remembered no more.
So surrender to Me, your whole self.
And you'll be a beautiful clay mold,
On this potter's heavenly display shelf.

1/4/2003

When God Speaks

When God speaks to us,
He uses many different means.
Wanting us to hear His voice,
He'll use anyway possible it seems.
Maybe a close friend,
Or just a great song.
Through a Pastors message,
You find you've done wrong.
Something you had seen,
While walking the mall.
Or could it have been,
A church member's phone call.
A strangers smiling face,
Or was it a baby's cry.
That set you to wondering,
God, you love me, but why!
Speaking through the spirit,
As we read His word.
Or that special nurse,
Your illness, helping to cure.
That beautiful flower,
You pass along the way.
The song the birds sing,
As they fly and play.
Whatever way God uses,
To speak to you.
Will you listen to His message,
And do what He asks you to?

1/15/03

Neal A. Carl

Climb Every Mountain

Climb every mountain,
One step at a time.
Stay focused on Jesus,
He is your safety line.

Just as you scale the mountain,
And you search for a good grip.
Hold on tightly in faith,
So your footing doesn't slip.

Keep looking up to heaven,
As you climb the mountain face.
Stand firm on Jesus the solid rock,
He'll help you finish the race.

With the faith of a tiny mustard seed,
We can move mountains great and small.
When our troubles become mountains,
With Jesus, we can overcome them all.

Jesus is the solid rock,
The foundation on which we stand.
Fear not, He's overcome this world,
And sits at God's right hand.

1/15/2003

Troubled by Storms

Has most of your life been troubled by storms?
Being tossed here and there by life's swarms.
Feeling like you can't ever gain any ground.
Being swallowed by the waves, something's pulling you down.
Can't seem to get things under control, or together.
Blown around by the wind, subject to the weather.
Feeling down and depressed, because it's cold and gray.
No sun in the sky, nothing good to say.
You feel so lost with nowhere to turn.
Everyone's plan for today, is your life to burn.
But there is someone, who cares for you and me.
He is an awesome GOD! He created all you see.
God's son Jesus cares too, so much He died on a cross.
For you and also for me, He died for all the lost!
He will calm the storms that trouble your life.
Fill you with His love; crush your pain and strife.
He will brighten your skies, put beautiful colors over gray.
He wants you to ask Him into your heart to stay.
Confess your sins to Him, tell Him of your pain.
He'll be there to help you each time you call upon His name.
Accept Jesus as Lord and give Him your praise.
He'll carry you through the storms, all of your days.

1/23/2003

Neal A. Carl

The Narrow Road

The narrow road,
Is rocky and rough.
And following Jesus,
Is sometimes tough.
Satan attacks you,
Without resting.
Looking for a weakness,
And always testing.
The closer you walk,
With the Lord Jesus.
The more Satan works,
To try and deceive us.
Many will fall if they,
Don't guard their heart.
Reading God's word daily,
Is a great place to start.
Pray to the Lord,
So you become stronger.
Use your shield of faith,
To battle on longer.
Jesus has already beaten,
Satan at the cross.
Fill your heart with God's word,
So you won't become lost.

1/24/2003

Seen My Scars

Have you seen my scars,
My nail pierced hands?
The cuts on my head,
From the thorn crown strands.
The hole in my side,
From the roman's spear.
My whip lashed back,
My flesh it did tear!
The suffering and pain,
And humiliation I took.
Open up your eyes,
I want you to look!
I didn't do this,
Just for me.
But to show my love,
Waiting for you to see!
I took the cross,
Dying in your place.
Accept my salvation,
Receive my Fathers grace.
I drank from my Fathers cup,
As only I could do.
Giving my body and blood,
All because I love you.
Open your heart,
And invite me in.
And I will cleanse you,
From all of your sin!

01/26/2003

Neal A. Carl

The Lighthouse

The history of the light house,
Goes back over one hundred years.
It warns approaching ships,
That shallow shoreline is near.
Whether it's a thick fog,
Or terrible stormy night.
The watchmen of the ship,
Watch for it's guiding light.
The lighthouse is used,
For warning ships large and small.
There may be danger ahead,
Listen for the foghorn call.
We as Christians also,
Have a guiding light.
And we are all special,
In the Lords sight.
Christ Jesus our Lord,
Is the one whom I speak!
He saves the lowly,
Lost and the weak.
Jesus told the Pharisees,
" I am the light of the world".
He'll withstand the crashing waves,
Any storm at the shore could hurl.
Jesus said, " whoever follows me,
Will have the light of life.
Never walking in darkness,"
Overcoming their pain and strife.
Jesus is the light of life,
A human lighthouse for all to see.
He's lighting the way to heaven,
Giving salvation to you and me.

01/26/2003

Sins Forgiven

I came to your world,
Born as a little child.
Given birth through a virgin,
So meek and mild.
My Father's great purpose,
I am here to do.
So you would worship Him,
With hearts made new.
I came to die on the cross,
For your sins pay the price.
I am the perfect lamb,
Slaughtered for your sacrifice.
I died to cleanse your sins,
No matter what they are.
I carried all your burdens,
My body marked by scars.
Confess your sins to me,
And they will be forgiven.
Ask me into your heart,
And I will quickly come in.
My Father's mercy and love,
I came here to show.
Your sins are forgiven,
To the world make me known.

02/02/2003

Neal A. Carl

My Love Overflows

Watch the waterfall,
See how it flows.
Where it started from,
No one really knows.

It's constant over pouring,
Never seems to end.
Water crashing at the bottom,
Mist to the air it does send.

My love is like a waterfall,
It's bountiful and overflowing.
You know where it comes from,
And each day, ever growing.

The mist in the air
That a waterfall makes,
Is like the Holy Spirit,
A new believer's heart over takes.

My love is much greater,
And soon you will know.
When you come to Heaven,
I will graciously show.

02/02/2003

28

My Temple

Your body is my temple,
When I dwell with-in your heart.
To give you a new foundation,
Is what I came into start.
Each day I work to make you,
A better person than you were before.
Cleansing you of your bad habits,
Giving you strength to sin no more.
I know part of you will fall,
And I will quickly come to repair.
That which had broken down,
I won't leave you in despair.
Each day I will forgive you,
When you confess your faults to me.
I want to beautify this temple,
For the entire world to see.
And because I live inside you,
It is me that you represent.
So when you speak to others,
They should see that you did repent.
The changes in you I make,
Will be seen by one and all.
So follow my direction closely,
I want others my name to call.

2/9/2003

Neal A. Carl

Reborn and Transformed

So you accepted Jesus,
As Savior and Lord.
Been forgiven of your sins,
To new life been reborn.

Washed by the blood,
Of God's only Son.
Now to be transformed,
The journey has begun.

Your old self must go,
That sinful life must die.
We must be more like Jesus,
No more should we lie.

To follow His prompting,
When He wants us to act.
He'll tell you what to say,
No need for public speaking or tact.

Just submit to the Spirit,
And follow His lead.
He'll take care of business,
Through us plant the seed.

Surrender to his changes,
As He transforms you.
Being blessed and amazed,
That you've been reborn- made new.

02/18/2003

Lost Cause or Saved!

Do you have feelings,
Of being a lost cause?
Like you have no value,
Death would be no loss.
No matter what you do,
It just doesn't go right.
What to do with yourself,
Seems to be your plight.
You want to give up,
But you still cling to life.
You've had all you can stand,
Can't take the pain and strife.
Let me tell you my friend.
Jesus Christ died for you!
He will change your life,
And live in your heart too.
There isn't anything you've done,
That he won't forgive you for.
Confess your sins to Him,
And open up your hearts door.
His spirit will encourage you,
And make a life saving change.
You'll be filled with joy,

As your life, He does rearrange.
Jesus died on the cross,
That was meant for you and me.
He covered our sins with His blood,
From Satan's grasp we've been set
free.
To Jesus you are priceless,
Great value- limit unknown.
Greater love for no man,
Could Jesus have shown.
Cast all your burdens,
And fears on the Lord.
He wants to save you,
And give blessings galore!
Before you know it,
You will be serving Him.
Helping others like you,
Turn from their sin.

2/19/2003

Neal A. Carl

Check Yourself

Are you living life,
The way you should?
Being cleansed from sin.
Was it really understood?

All your past sins,
Have been washed away.
But you should not,
In that life stay!

When Jesus died on the cross,
He covered your sins with his blood.
You have been washed clean,
Removing all your sinful mud.

And now each day,
We should be like Him.
Living life as he did,
Rebuking all chance to sin.

Striving to live Holy lives,
Keeping our thoughts focused above.
Helping those in need,
With compassion and love.

So read God's word daily,
And heed to His teaching.
Do not continue to sin,
Holy living continue seeking!

02/22/2003

Refer to Galatians 5: 16-26

A Matter of Time

Just when did time start,
And how long will it go?
Only God has the answer,
This, Jesus has told us so.

Our life on this earth,
Is just a matter of time.
We should be preaching Jesus,
Not walking around blind.

From one moment to the next,
Just where will you be?
Living your life for Jesus,
A good witness for all to see?

One day real soon,
We'll be in our heavenly home.
And we will be questioned,
Before Almighty God's throne.

Just what did you do,

To spread the gospel news.
Jesus is for all people,
The Gentiles and the Jews.

Did you just waste time,
Thinking about self or lying around?
Or were you seeking the lost,
So their salvation could be found?

In God's word Jesus said,
"I don't know when I'll be back."
"Father God is in charge of time,"
And it's time that you lack!

So don't waste that time,
Making excuses for yourself.
Seek out the lost people,
They all need Jesus help!

3/03/2003

33

Neal A. Carl

Life Goes On

So just where do you go,
After your body dies?
Will you go to heaven,
Or down where hell lies?

There are so many people,
Who have this belief.
That when they die,
They'll feel no more grief.

This is true for those who,
Are washed by the blood,
Of Jesus our Lord:
God's one and only son.

But what of those,
Who have rejected Jesus.
Or haven't heard about,
God's loving gift for us?

Do people have any idea,
Can they really understand?
There is a living soul,
With-in each woman and man.

A soul that lives on,
After the body is dead.
There is life in Jesus,
Or with Satan instead.

The choice must be made,
By people young and old.
You can't get to heaven,
By works, no tickets are sold!

There is only one way,
To be sure of your fate.
Accept Jesus as Savior,
Before it's too late!

3/03/2003

Neal A. Carl

Show My Love

Go out into the world,
And show them my love.
Teach them about me,
And my father above.

Shower them with kindness,
Help meet their needs.
Reflect that I'm in you,
By your words and deeds.

Give them some clothing,
And needed food to eat.
Help them with problems,
Pray for those you meet.

Offer them some shelter,
If you possibly can.
Help them to walk when,
They are too weak to stand.

Drive them to the doctors,
Should they need to go.
Helping them with errands,
My love to show.

There are so many people,
We can help in so many ways.
Even read to a shut-in,
To help brighten their days.

When I give you the chance,
By opening up doors.
Do it with a joyful heart,
Not just as more chores.

3/4/2003

Feeling Condemned

Do you have those feelings,
That you've been condemned?
Your past is so sinful,
No help could one recommend.

So lost and alone,
No where to turn.
Can't help but wonder,
What lesson didn't I learn?

Too much confusion,
More than you can bear.
Sometimes you find yourself,
In the lost in space stare.

Just who can you turn to,
To whom can you go?
What you've been through,
Who else would know?

Jesus has been there,
Just waiting for your call.

He's experienced all things,
And can help you through all.

He died for your sake,
To wash away your sins.
Asking Him into your heart,
It's then the healing begins.

He'll lift you up,
Give you strength for each day.
Walk along side you,
When troubles come your way.
So put your trust in the Lord,
He really does love you.
You'll experience great joy,
As you are made new.

3/4/2003

Neal A. Carl

Broken the Law

You've committed some sins,
And broken God's law.
Found out you are human,
And that you have a flaw.

Whether you know what you did,
Or they just crept up on you.
You always were a sinner,
The Bible tells us this truth.

There is only one way,
To be forgiven your sin.
Confess them to Jesus,
Ask Him into your heart to live.

For all have sinned and,
Fallen short of God's glory.
God's word tells us so,
This is not someone's story.

So now accept the fact,
You can't change on your own.
The Holy Spirit must be in you,
To put away those faults shown.

We must grow in the Lord,
A new life should we live.
Empowered by the Holy Spirit,
Put to death a life of sin.

3/5/2003

Your Turn Now

You've accepted Jesus and,
Now you're sin free.
Been given new life,
For all to see.

Now you must grow,
And with Jesus walk.
Grow in his word,
Think before you talk.

Each day you'll be molded,
And shown how to live.
He'll cast off bad habits,
Like sand through a sieve.

The changes He makes,
Are better by far.
As He shapes who,
You really are.

Soon you'll serve Him,
And He'll tell you where to go.
So that others like you,
Jesus as Savior they come to know.

03/05/2003

39

Neal A. Carl

Will You Obey?

If I ask,
Will you obey?
Follow my leading,
Throughout each day?

When I give you prompting,
To go out and serve.
Will you accept the task,
Or just loose your nerve?

Sometimes I'll ask for,
Your financial aid.
Or maybe to pray,
That revivals are made.

To go out and teach,
Throughout the land.
Or be a source of comfort,
Give someone a helping hand.

To grow in the spirit,
You must do what I ask.
I will lift you up,
And sustain you for the task.

I'll give you gifts,
So you can serve me.
They'll be blessings for you,
Glory and honor I'll receive.

So obey my prompting,
We'll have a closer walk.
The closer we become,
The more we will talk.

3/9/2003

What's Next?

You've accepted the Gospel,
Confessed all your sins.
Asked Jesus into your heart,
And your new life begins.

So what happens next,
Where do I go from here?
Ask the spirit for direction,
Your path He'll help steer.

Read His word daily,
Be in continual prayer.
Listen for His voice,
His message he will share.

As you strive to learn,
And grow in the spirit.
God will challenge you to,
Reach out, so others hear it.

Great things to you,
The spirit will impart.
As He continues to grow,
Within your heart.

As you learn to trust more,
And feed upon God's word.
You'll be blessed beyond measure,
Your broken heart cured.

So don't stand there and wonder,
Just what do I do next.
Pick up God's word,
Pray and read the text.

3/9/2003

41

Neal A. Carl

Sheltered in the Lord

As you walk through,
The valley's of life.
Feeling lost and alone,
Overcome by pain and strife.

How can anyone handle,
So much death and despair?
Put your trust in the Lord,
Love with you, He'll share.

Sheltered in the Lord,
Is where you can be.
When ugliness in this world,
Is all you can see.

We ourselves are very weak,
Temptations are always strong.
Sheltered in God's arms,
Is where we belong.

When you feel the need,
To hide from your fears.
Put your faith in Jesus,
He is always very near.

Stay **sheltered in the Lord**,
As each day comes and goes.
Because your very future,
God has seen and knows.

3/14/2003

When Temptation Comes

As you wake each day,
And seek out the Lord.
Put on your shield of faith,
Study His word-your sword.

As your day progresses,
The temptations may become stronger.
Trust in the Lord Jesus,
For courage to battle on longer.

Whoever your foe may be,
Or however hard the task.
Jesus is there to help you,
He's just waiting for you to ask.

So pray in the spirit,
Seek out his direction.
Don't go it alone,
And loose your faith connection.

When we walk with the Lord,
And face our trials with Him.
He is faithful to forgive,
When we fall to sin.

But to overcome the trials,
That we face each day.
We must stay focused on Him,
So we can hear what He has to say.

3/15/2003

Neal A. Carl

Overpowered by Fear

Are you living a life,
Over powered by fear?
Afraid that any moment,
Harm or death is near.
You tip-toe around,
Who lurks over there?
You get even more jumpy,
With every noise you hear.
The evils of this world,
Give you such a fright!
So many thoughts of fear,
You can't even sleep at night.
Everywhere you look,
No matter where you turn.
Dealing with your fears,
Is a hard lesson to learn.
Although these worldly fears,
May be hard for you to conquer.
Your fear of death in sin,
Forgiveness from Jesus will cure.
Jesus shed his blood,
At the cross of Calvary.
Cleansing us of our sins,
Death from sin, been set free.
Jesus is there waiting for you,
To ask Him into your heart.
Confessing your sins to Him,
His forgiveness will then start.
You'll soon overcome your fears,
As the Holy Spirit grows with in you.
No more fearing death in this world,
You'll be home in heaven soon!

3/16/2003

No More Pain

For those of you who suffer,
Each day with physical pain.
Reading God's word and praying,
Have been cleansed of the sinful stain.

Take comfort in your knowing,
Jesus will return for you!
And when we get to heaven,
We will have new bodies too!

Enduring pain will be no more,
No more sorrow to bring us tears.
Never again to face death,
Or deal with earthly fears.

We will be home with Jesus,
Being showered with His love,
Reunited with God's family,
Our loved ones now with God above.

Walls of gem and pearly gates,
And streets of transparent gold.
All lit up with God's glory,
This in God's word we are told!

This revelation given to John,
By Jesus, God's only son.
Our only way to life eternal,
There isn't another one!

3/16/2003

Neal A. Carl

Are You Listening?

I walked among you,
For so many years.
Healing the sick,
Calming your fears.

To many I ministered,
And performed great miracles.
I died on the cross,
A criminals death of spectacles.

I rose from the death,
And appeared to hundreds.
Showed you all my scars,
I'm alive, just as I said!

What more can I do,
To show you my love?
I'm even preparing a place,
For you in heaven above.

I speak to you in my word,

And my spirit convicts you.
Why aren't you listening,
I want to give life a new.

I have tried to teach,
You so many lessons.
To change your ways,
And give you directions.

I want you to know,
That I really do care.
And want a relationship,
We can both share.

So pray and study my word,
I want you to see.
You need to listen more,
To walk closer with me!

3/22/2003

What If?

What would you think,
If I just didn't care?
Only thinking of myself,
My life I did spare.

Didn't heal the sick,
Or care for the blind.
So mean to all people,
No compassion of any kind.

Judging you one and all,
Your faults I did tell.
Offering no plan of salvation,
From the gates of hell.

No freedom from your sins,
They just grew like a boil.
And your body just festered,
Like burns from hot oil.

But I love you completely!

So be of great cheer!
I am your salvation,
You have nothing to fear.

I did heal the sick,
And made the blind to see.
And died on the cross,
So you would be free.

My love for you,
Is greater than you know.
My death on that cross,
Should have told you so.

So follow me my friend,
Pick up your cross!
Cast off the, what if,
Witness to the lost!

3/22/2003

Neal A. Carl

Praise the Lord

Praise the Lord,
In heart-felt song.
When things are good,
And when they go wrong.

Praise the Lord,
For the beautiful day.
In all you do,
Every word you say.

Praise Him for your,
Food from the ground.
The death He died,
Your salvation found.

Praise the Lord,
For His written word.
And for messages preached,
That you have heard.

Thank Him for his miracles,
Answered prayers of the past.
For His guidance of the future,
His love will forever last.

Praise Him in every thought,
For your every need.
Give Him praise as,
You do every deed.

Our risen Lord,
Deserves our praise.
With hearts of love,
To Him our hands raise.

3/27/2003

48

Jesus is Coming

Has anyone ever told you?
Did you refuse to hear?
Jesus is coming soon,
His time of glory is near!

The trumpet will soon sound,
And Jesus will appear!
Whether you were saved,
The answer will be clear!

I tell you this truth!
" You should have no doubt."
Confess Jesus as Lord,
Praise Him with a shout!

Spread the news to others,
No one should be left behind.
We can't make the decision,
Forcing their change of mind.

But we do need to tell them,
And the love of Jesus show.
Jesus died for all people,
This they need to know.

Jesus is coming soon,
We're running out of time.
His blood was shed for all sins,
Not just for yours and mine.

3/16/2003

Neal A. Carl

A Prayer by Jesus

Father please forgive them,
They do not understand.
To follow me completely,
They must make a stand.

Leave the past life behind,
Be molded to life a new.
Releasing all of their bad habits,
Not restricting me to a few.

For them to follow me,
Go and do what I say.
They must surrender completely,
So I can show them my way.

They should stop being so stubborn,
Let me turn their lives around.
Changing what is needed,
Setting them on solid ground.

I don't want their love,
Only when it's best for them.
I want it always,
Even when faced with problems.

Give me more time father,
Grant me what I ask.
So more lost are found,
To help complete the task.

3/21/2003

Seeds of Faith

Wherever you go,
Throughout each day.
We should reflect Jesus,
In all we do and say.

Jesus uses us,
To plant the seeds.
With those we talk to,
And assist with their needs.

When we tell someone,
What Jesus has done.
The changes in our life,
That He has begun.

But for these faith seeds,
To be firmly planted.
We must serve focused on Jesus,
And take nothing for granted.

Some people will watch,
Just to see if we fall.
Following you closely,
Hoping you hit a wall.

So the next time you're given,
Seeds of faith to instill.
Make sure that in all things,
You are doing God's will!

4/2/2003

Neal A. Carl

Hourglass Design

This is an observation,
Of the hour glass design.
The sand flowing top to bottom,
Is how it's used to tell time.

But if you take a moment,
And watch the sand fall.
The top glass soon empties,
As the other holds all.

This example will suggest,
As we give all to Jesus.
The sand leaving the top,
Is the Spirit filling us.

As the sand collects,
In the bottom glass.
No more room for sin,
The Spirit fills it's mass.

So look at the hour glass,
And flip it around.
As your sinful life disappears,
A Spirit filled life is found!

4/2/2003

Stand Together

Standing together on the solid rock,
This we are called to do.
We as Christ's building block,
Are His foundation made new.

For His message to spread,
We must band together.
Standing against the waves of Satan,
God will control the weather.

The strength we all need,
For the completion of the task.
Will come from our Lord,
All we need to do is ask.

When the church unites,
In the service of our Lord.
The blessing of winning many new,
Lost souls will be scored!

So answer our Savior's call,
Together we will stand.
The fields are full and ripe,
And the harvest is at hand.

4/6/03

Neal A. Carl

He Has Risen

Jesus came into Jerusalem,
Knowing what was ahead.
That He would be crucified,
And rise again from the dead.

Even though He in fact was God,
He didn't hesitate to drink the cup.
Humiliated by spit and beaten,
His flesh was whipped and cut up.

He died for the sins,
Of all people on earth.
This was His great purpose,
From His very birth.

He suffered and died,
Because He loved us so much.
He could have come off that cross,
Called on His angels in the clutch.

But He did it all,
And passed through Satan's prison.
Just as He promised,
He Has Risen!

4/6/03

Worship Me!

I know that there are,
Things that you need.
But you should never allow,
That need to turn into greed.

I will take great care,
In answering your prayers.
But Satan will tempt you,
So I caution you, beware!

I have given you so much,
And I want you to worship me.
I am an awesome God!
I created all you see.

I have even given you,
Some of the material things.
A car and home, food, clothes,
But how much happiness did they bring?

I can fulfill your request,
Even all your hearts desire.
But ask according to my will,
Worship me, that's what I require!

4/7/03

Neal A. Carl

I Have Risen

I came into your world,
With one mission in mind.
I also healed the sick,
The paralyzed and the blind.

I came to cleanse the sins,
And give forgiveness to all mankind.
But you must confess them to me,
And ask me, to come live inside.

That death on the cross,
I endured that for you.
I bled and died,
And rose from the grave too!

I told my disciples,
So that they already knew.
This had to happen,
And that my words were true.

The Angel rolled away the stone,
And then told the women.
That just as I said,
I broke the chains of Satan's prison.

He didn't have the power,
Nor was it his decision.
I am Christ the Lord!
And I Have Risen!

4/26/2003

Out of Control

Have you ever felt,
Lost and out of control?
Like you are falling,
Through a black hole.

You try so hard,
To get a grip.
But your life has,
Through your fingers slipped.

You thought you could handle,
All trials that came along.
Then you get frustrated,
When things go all wrong.

You cry out for help,
But when will it come?
You've looked every where,
And couldn't find anyone.

Now you have determined,
It's the end of your rope.
Everything's out of control,
And you've lost all hope.

With nowhere to turn,
You surrender, then pray.
Asking Jesus for help,
To show you the way.

Now trust in Him,
To meet your need.
Give Jesus total control,
And you will succeed.

5/2/2003

Neal A. Carl

It's Your Choice

When you walk with the Lord,
You still have freedom of choice.
Will you follow the world's way,
Or listen and obey Jesus' voice?

When he asks you to serve,
Maybe even in harms way.
Will you answer the call,
Or in the whale's belly stay?

If it's the chosen task,
That you really fear.
Ask Jesus for strength,
And He will be near.

When the door opens to witness,
With whom God wants you to speak.
Will you, without reservation,
Humble yourself and God's will seek?

If chosen for a position,
With in your local church.
Will you accept and serve well,
Ending the committee's search?

In so many ways,
God can use us all.
Will you obey God's leading,
Or to Satan's trap fall?

You have the freedom,
Which will you choose?
Surrender all and obey God,
Or fall to Satan, and self-loose?

5/5/2003

A Sinner's Testimony

I grew up in the church,
And was taught how to live.
Even though I became saved,
I thought that was all I had to give.
I went through my early years,
With the best of intentions.
But I fell so much to sin,
There weren't any honorable mentions.
So many of my friends,
Gave me this false hope.
It's okay to continue in sin,
You're not under a microscope.
No one really cares,
If you continue to do wrong.
As long as you know Jesus,
And to Him you belong.
But Jesus said once forgiven,
We should walk in holy living.
That our character will change,
And strive to overcome sinning.
We should no longer walk,
In the path we once took.
Jesus must shine through us,
Giving us that holy look.
By the way we act,
And the path we walk.
The world must see Jesus,
Even in the manner we talk.
Actions do speak more loudly,
Than any words we can say.
Witness by a living example,
Walk with Jesus today!

5/8/2003

Neal A. Carl

This is the Day

When God opens the door,
For you to spread the word.
Don't go running away,
So the message isn't heard.

This is the day when,
They will hear the good news.
And God wants you to respond,
Not start singing the blues.

Surrender to his will,
And seize the day.
The Lord will give you,
The words you need to say.

The seed will be planted,
And the Spirits moving show.
That by answering God's call,
Others His Son, will come to know.

We must stay focused on God,
And stay on His plan.
This is the day to witness,
To every child, woman, and man.

5/25/2003

One Victory at a Time

When you're going through those tough changes,
That God is making in your life.
Carving away those bad habits like a butcher,
Slicing the fat off the meat with His knife.

To shape us into perfection,
Removing our sinful slime.
God is guiding us through,
One victory at a time.

Each time a sinful habit,
Becomes part of our history.
God's grace to overcome each one,
Gives us one more victory.

God is faithful and just,
To forgive us each sin.
And **one victory at a time,**
Is the best place to begin.

So don't get so frustrated,
Thinking the changes are too slow.
Let God control the progress,
Your faithful heart will surely grow.

5/26/2003

Neal A. Carl

Do It His Way

As we live each day,
And we interact with others.
We should reflect our Lord Jesus,
As we deal with our sisters and brothers.

In each situation,
We should seek God in prayer.
To do it His way,
And of Satan's temptation beware.

We know that each day,
Has many forked roads.
Doing it His way,
Will ease our burden loads.

Jesus overcame the world,
Doing things God's way.
Stay focused on Him,
You'll conquer temptation today!

5/27/2003

Your Mission

When you accept Jesus,
As your Lord and Savior.
He begins to make changes,
Preparing a Holy behavior.

Our past is now clean,
Because we've been reborn.
To prepare for your mission,
You must now be transformed.

Each day of our life,
We are to serve and witness.
Telling those we meet,
About God's plan of forgiveness.

Jesus instructed His disciples,
And gave them the great commission.
Share the gospel with the world,
This is also your great mission.

By the way you and I live,
This is what the world will see.
We must reflect Jesus in all things,
Children of God, forgiven and free!

6/4/2003

Neal A. Carl

No Time to Waste

The end is very near,
There is no time to waste.
The Lord is coming soon,
Spread the gospel with haste.

God doesn't want anyone,
To die in their sin.
We must tell all about Jesus,
It is time to begin.

The days are getting short,
Today could be the last.
We need to get busy,
Don't let a moment get past.

It could be today or,
Maybe, even tomorrow.
We must use every opportunity,
Because time, we cannot barrow.

When the Lord stops it,
That will be the end!
No more time to witness,
The unsaved to hell He'll send!

6/7/2003

Whose Choice Is It?

Is it up to you and I,
Whose soul the Lord will save?
Was it you or I whose life
On that cross for sins gave?

Are we asked our opinion,
When we're told to witness?
It's no choice of ours,
Who God grants forgiveness.

We are commanded to serve,
And go where God leads.
He knows the hearts of all,
And also their very needs.

Your life will be blessed,
When you do God's will.
Answer His call without question,
Your missions, with joy fulfill.

6/9/2003

Neal A. Carl

God's Written Word

Did you read,
Your Bible today?
To read what the Spirit,
Of God had to say?

To give you direction,
For your day of trial.
Helping you travel,
The narrow road of survival.

The message is the same,
Always relevant with time.
The Bible speaks to your heart,
As it does to mine.

Though the passage is the same,
Its meaning may not be.
As you read God's word daily,
New truths you will see.

What God reveals to me,
Maybe different for you.
Either way God is telling us,
What He wants us to do.

So read God's word always,
And seek His will.
The storms in your life,
He will quiet and still.

6/13/2003

Simple Blessings

I gave you rain,
That waters the earth.
Then germinated the seeds,
Giving the plants rebirth.

So many food sources,
For you to eat.
From the sea and soil,
Also animals for meat.

The sun for daylight,
Beautiful skies of blue.
Pleasing scents of nature,
Everyday is new.

Multicolored trees and flowers,
That cover the ground.
Birds of all sizes,
Making sweet cheerful sound.

When the days get hot,
I cause the wind to blow.
These are simple blessings,
Of my creation to show.

I care for the birds,
But I love you much more.
I want to shower you with blessings,
More than grains of sand along the shore.

All these simple blessings,
You experience every day.
Are yours without asking,
I lovingly give them away.

6/14/2003

Neal A. Carl

What A Day!

The trumpet sounds,
And our Lord appears!
The sky filled with His glory,
Our eyes fill with joyful tears!

The burning in our hearts,
As we hear Jesus say;
" Come with me my child."
Praise the Lord, **what a day!**

As we rise to meet Him,
And look into His face.
Stumbling for words to say,
Jesus gives us a warm embrace.

"Well done my child,
Come along with me.
I've prepared a place for you,
Now together we'll always be."

We'll sit down and talk,
Go walking side by side.
Great will be that day,
When Jesus comes for His bride!

8/2/2003

The Battle is Over

You've walked with Jesus,
Along the narrow road.
Facing all of life's challenges,
Sharing the burden load.

You've been a good servant,
And finished the race.
Now you're tired and weary,
Waiting to see Jesus' face.

Your body is aging,
And getting too weak.
That homeward call from Jesus,
Is now what you seek.

The battle is over!
Your time is at hand!
Soon you'll meet Jesus,
Up in Glory Land!

8/8/2003

Neal A. Carl

The Gift of Love

The gift of love,
Comes into your heart.
He's not some fantasy,
Or great work of art.
This gift of love,
Is everlasting!
Not some special spell,
That cupid is casting.
He fills your heart,
With love overflowing.
His spirit with in you,
Never stops growing.
This kind of relationship,
No human can sever,
Jesus will live in your heart,
And stay with you forever.
He'll walk with you,
And guide you each day.
You'll conquer your fears,
As you follow His way.
This gift of love,
Is God's Son Jesus!
He'll change our hearts,
And the way the world sees us.
Walking with Jesus,
Each day is a blessing.
As He reveals to us,
The sins that need confessing.
Just where can you find,
This great gift of love?
He's Jesus, God's Son,
That's whom I speak of!
Confess your sins to Him,
And claim Jesus as Lord!
You'll receive life everlasting,
Death in sin, fear no more!

8/9/2003

Do You Remember?

Do you remember,
Who you used to be?
Hiding in the darkness,
Feelings of guilt, you didn't see.
Not realizing the hurt,
You caused your loved ones?
As you continued to sin,
Thinking it's so much fun.
Then in a Moment...
You hit a great wall!
It was someone special,
Who answered God's call!
They showed you love,
And you began to talk.
Finding they have a savior,
With whom they walk.
Your heart began to burn,
Tears well up in your eyes.
As they tell you of Jesus,
And answer your questions, why!
They told you of God's,
Great plan of salvation!

And how with Jesus,
You can share this relation.

Do you remember,
The changes He made?
Your heart was cleansed,
Of the sins He waived.
That burning desire,
God's witness did show.
Introduced you to Jesus,
And Jesus you now know!
Do you remember how,
Jesus changed your life?
Then go, become a witness.
Bring someone to
Jesus Christ!!

8/9/2003

71

Neal A. Carl

Monster Slayer

Do you have addictions,
To drugs and alcohol?
Or is sexual temptation,
The vice to which you fall?
Do you frequently lie,
To cover your tracks?
Or some other bad habits,
Non-mentioned devilish acts?
Do you have monsters,
In your life that you fear?
Your faith is shaken,
Whenever they appear?
You doubt your ability,
Thinking you can't cope.
Have those lost feelings,
Like there's no hope.
Let me tell you my friend.
There's no need to live this way!
Jesus Christ died for you!
Call out to Him today!
He'll help you overcome,
Those monstrous addictive trials.
He'll stay close beside you,
No matter how many miles!
Jesus is the monster slayer,
And those monstrous trials destroy!
He'll take your troubled life,
And fill it with courage and joy!

8/9/2003

72

Answer the Call

So many times you,
Maybe asked to serve.
Will you answer the call,
Or just loose your nerve?

Afraid of the task,
Or that you might fail?
With low esteem or faith.
Satan will prevail.

We must surrender ourselves,
To our Lord Jesus Christ!
Take up our cross,
And not think twice.

The Lord has told us,
We'll never walk alone.
His spirit lives in us,
Our direction to be shown.

Stay focused on Jesus,
As you answer the call.
He'll walk along side you,
Giving you strength, not to fall.

9/2/2003

About the Author

Neal Allan Carl was raised in a Christian family. He received Jesus as Lord and Savior at age seven and was baptized in his Baptist Church. As he grew in the Lord, he served in many capacities there. Sunday School Assistant Superintendent. Christian Education Committee Member, and Deacon.

In August 1988, God called Neal into Jail Ministry as a Corrections Officer. These past 15 years, Neal spread God's message to the inmates as God led. Many of them accepted Jesus as Lord and Savior. These experiences have brought him to a closer walk with God, and the inspiration of these poems of God's guidance.

Neal, praises God for this Poem Ministry opportunity and blessing.

Printed in the United States
37799LVS00009B/55-57